LITTLE EXERCISE BOOKS

Brain games for personal wellbeing

EXERCISES FOR

SELF-ESTEEM

Rosette Poletti & Barbara Dobbs

Illustrations Jean Augagneur

The Five Mile Press

The Five Mile Press Pty Ltd
1 Centre Road, Scoresby
Victoria 3179 Australia
www.fivemile.com.au

This edition published 2012, Reprinted 2012
First published 2008 by
Éditions Jouvence, S.A.
Chemin du Guillon 20
Case 184
CH-1233 Bernex
www.editions-jouvence.com
info@editions-jouvence.com

Cover and page layout: Éditions Jouvence
Cover and internal illustrations: Jean Augagneur
except the illustrations of the maze (p. 13),
the Tibetan endless knot (p. 33), the mandala (p. 39)
and the wild roses (pp. 22 and 48)
reworked or illustrated by Barbara Dobbs
The flowers are taken from Les harmonisants émotionnels
du Dr Bach, Barbara Dobbs, Recto-Verseau, Romont, 2006
Translated into English by Patsy Abott-Charles
Formatting in English translation: Caz Brown

ISBN: 978 1 74300 271 1

Printed in China

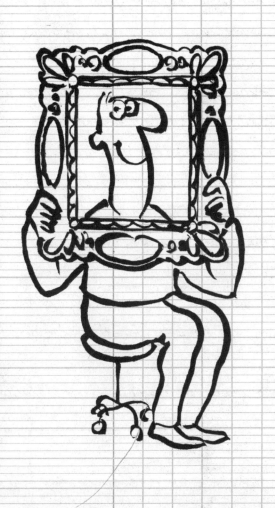

Have you been bewildered by the title of this exercise book? Welcome! Self-esteem is one of the essential sources of the joy of living, it enables you to feel comfortable with yourself, to like yourself and like others. It can be developed all through your life. That's why we suggest starting right now.

3

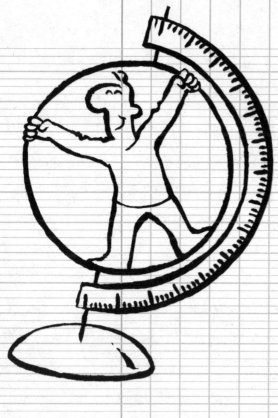

Well, you're there, somewhere on this planet. You are a human being among billions of others! But you are unique, irreplacable. Because before you there has never been another human being exactly like you, with the same experiences of life, the same skills and the same genetic base. This means that you are extraordinarily precious! Only you can live your life, only you can bring to the universe everything that you are, everything that you know.

To be able to be all that you are and bring to this planet all that you can, you need to benefit from good self-esteem.

This little exercise has been put together to help you to develop this vital trait.

Carry it with you and do the exercises suggested in it. Above all, take pleasure in it; that is our wish.

Self-esteem

'Throughout the universe there isn't another person who exactly resembles me. I'm me and everything that I am is unique. I am responsible for myself, I have everything I need in the here and now to have a full life. I can choose to show what's best in me, I can choose to love, to be competent, to find a sense to my life and an order in the universe. I can choose to develop myself, to believe in and to live in harmony with myself, with other people and with God. I deserve to be accepted and loved exactly as I am, here and now. I like and accept myself, I decide to live fully from today on.'

— Virginia Satir

5

Self-esteem

Self-confidence

Assertiveness

Self-image

Ideal self

Concept of oneself

? ? ?

One can't make
head nor tail of it!

A few short definitions to clarify it for you!

• Self-esteem

This is the result of how a person regards him or herself: on physical appearence, on skills, on professional success, on the richness of emotional life. Success in one or other of these areas doesn't guarantee self-esteem. That's the result of a balance between each of these different aspects. Self-esteem is a delicate and changeable asset. When we live a life that respects our own values, self-esteem increases, but it decreases every time our behaviour is contrary to ourselves.

· **Self-confidence**

This exists in a person's spirit, believing that you have the means to face any kind of situation.

· **Assertiveness**

This is the ability to take your place with kindness and firmness amongst others, to communicate clearly and to accept and refuse.

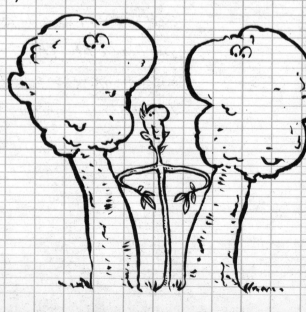

- **Self-image**

  How you see yourself.

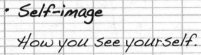

- **Ideal self**

  How you would like to be.

- **Concept of you**

  This is the total view of
  yourself: self-image, ideal
  self and self-esteem.

9

Self-esteem can be summed up in two major statements:

· The perception of personal ability

· The inner conviction of having value as a person

This definition of self-esteem requires you to be able to:

· Accept yourself for what you are

· Control your emotions

· Conduct your affairs with others

· Face up to conflicts

· Accept things as they are (reality)

· Assert yourself with others

· Have confidence in yourself

What sort of estimation of yourself do you have?

1. I accept myself as a person.
   ☐ never   ☐ sometimes   ☐ often   ☑ always

2. I am self-confident.
   ☑ never   ☐ sometimes   ☐ often   ☐ always

3. I can assert myself.
   ☐ never   ☑ sometimes   ☐ often   ☐ always

4. I like most people.
   ☐ never   ☐ sometimes   ☑ often   ☐ always

5. I can express myself easily in a group.
   ☐ never   ☐ sometimes   ☑ often   ☐ always

6. I deserve to be happy.
   ☐ never   ☐ sometimes   ☐ often   ☑ always

7. I consider that my opinion is as important as the opinion of others.
   ☐ never   ☐ sometimes   ☐ often   ☑ always

8. 'It's human to make mistakes'; do you say this to yourself when you make a mistake?
   ☐ never   ☑ sometimes   ☐ often   ☐ always

9. Is it easy for you to listen to a justified criticism of something you've done?
   ☐ never   ☑ sometimes   ☐ often   ☐ always

10. Are you able to tell another adult that you don't accept their behaviour?
    ☐ never   ☑ sometimes   ☐ often   ☐ always

11. When a relationship is no longer sustainable, can you end it?
    ☐ never   ☑ sometimes   ☐ often   ☐ always

12. Can you say 'no' when it's necessary?
    ☐ never   ☐ sometimes   ☑ often   ☐ always

$$\frac{\begin{array}{r}6\\6\\5\end{array}}{17}$$

11

Each time you ticked **'always'**,
that counts for 3 points (36 points in all).

Each time you ticked **'often'**,
that counts for 2 points.

Each time you ticked **'sometimes'**,
that counts for 1 point.

Each time you ticked **'never'**,
you get no points.

Results:

0-15 points: You have obstacles to overcome. You're going to win new points as you work through this exercise book. Your life will become easier!

16-25 points: You are on the way. You just need to develop a few important points.

26-36 points: You already have a good estimation of yourself! In finding ways to improve, you will always find greater pleasure living amongst others.

To rest your spirit a little, we suggest that you relax by walking around (with the point of a pencil) the maze of the cathedral of Our Lady at Amiens (France). You need to follow the black lines.

How to build your self-esteem

You have to build realtionships with others: first of all with your parents, then family, friends, teachers — everyone who can have an influence on the perception of the person that is you.

14

Who has participated in developing your self-esteem.
Draw the important people who have communicated
positive messages to you. Write their messages at
the end of the lines. For example, Uncle Paul: 'You
have got everything necessary for success!'

ME

Mum - I love you so much
You're so talented

Eamonn
You're work is fabulous

15

Who has communicated negative messages to you th___
destroyed your estimation of yourself?

• Draw these people and write their messages at the e___
  of the lines. For example, my first kindergarten teach___
  Mrs Martin, who repeatedly said: 'Are you complete___
  stupid or what?'

Now, cross out these destructive messages with a big black marker. And on this page write positive messages to replace them. For example: 'You are a very alert child! I like teaching you all sorts of things!' As Mrs Martin has long since retired, you can change the message in this way.

...

...

...

...

...

...

...

...

...

...

...

...

...

...

Depending on the messages received from those who raised you, you may have a negative perception of yourself because that's what happens; it's these messages in our childhood that imprint themselves on us and become our internal dialogue.

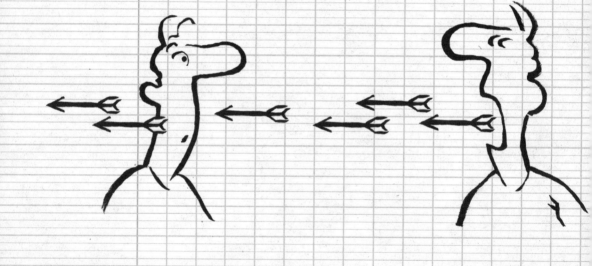

What is your perception of yourself?

1. Does criticism from others hurt you?
   - ☑ yes   ☐ no

2. Do you dread new experiences?
   - ☑ yes   ☑ no

3. Do you speak to others about your personal successes?
   - ☐ yes   ☑ no

4. Do you try to make others responsible for your mistakes?
   - ☐ yes   ☑ no

5. Do you have a tendency to be too timid or aggressive?
   - ☑ yes   ☐ no

6. Do you try to hide your feelings?
   - ☐ yes   ☑ no

7. Are you ashamed of your physical appearance?
   - ☑ yes   ☑ no

8. Do you feel better when others fail?
   - ☐ yes   ☑ no

9. Are you comfortable with close relationships with others?
   - ☑ yes   ☐ no

10. Do you find excuses not to change?
    - ☑ yes   ☐ no

19

If you've answered **yes** to most of these questions, then you need to improve your perception of yourself.

How do you acquire bad self-esteem?

Contrary to what you may think, it isn't just by saying to a child that he/she is marvellous that good self-esteem will be acquired. Self-control and discipline are also fundamental to self-esteem.

Here are some factors that can disrupt development of self-esteem:

· Overprotection by parents, grandparents and older brothers and sisters

✗ Words that wound

✗ Not having enough attention paid to you by others

✗ Continual criticism

✗ Losing heart and giving up in the face of difficulties

· Expecting too much

✗ Inconsistent self-discipline

✗ Physical abuse

· Scholastic failure

Did you experience any of the things listed on the previous page when you were a child? Which ones?

...

...

...

...

'The important thing is not what
has been done to us, but how we
react to what has been done to us.'

— Jean-Paul Sartre

If you have experienced some disruption of the development of your self-esteem, what have you done about it?

· Have you been able to try to understand the other person(s) or forgive your parents? Or look at the matter in another way?

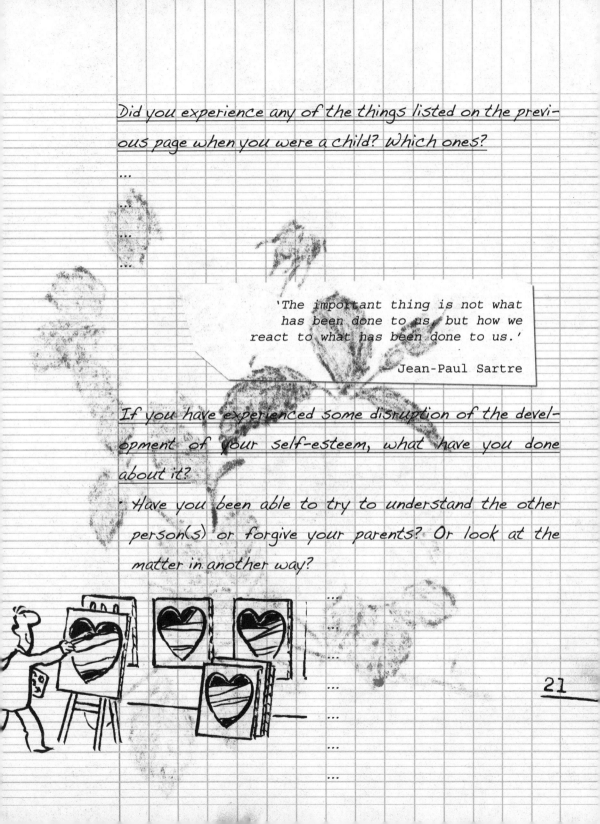

...

...

...

...

...

...

The eglantine, the wild rose that flowers everywhere, is a symbol of self-esteem. Take the time to colour in these flowers!

Dare to be yourself

Depending on the importance of the disruptions suffered during education, a person may try to hide who he/she is from others, for fear of not being accepted. It reaches the point where the person doesn't know who he or she really is. A better knowledge of yourself helps relationships with others and improves one's self-esteem.

In the sixties, two researchers, Joseph Luft and Harry Ingham, developed a model that they called *The window of Johari*. It showed the evolution of communication between two people. It helps to demonstrate the evolution of self-esteem.

The public face
What I know about myself and I show to others.

The blind zone
What I don't know about myself, but others do.

The hidden face
What I know about myself and I hide from others.

The unknown
What neither I nor others know about me (the unconscious).

When you develop your self-esteem, you can improve the entry in the quadrant headed '**hidden face**'. This happens because you increase confidence in yourself and in others.

The '**blind zone**' reduces because of your openness to others and their opinions increase your knowledge of yourself.

It's also possible that '**unknown**' will reduce because the unconscious finds ways of expressing itself.

The public face	The blind zone
What do you show to others?	What can you ask from those you know concerning what they see in you?
The hidden face	The unknown
What hidden aspects of you could you show to others?	Do you talk about your dreams? Do you write them down?

Self-esteem and relationships with others (positions of life)

Eric Berne, founder of Transactional Analysis, working with Franklin Ernst, described four ways in which to understand how we position ourselves in relation to others, and these are a direct reflection of our self-esteem.

He called these ways 'positions of life'.

They depend on the perception we have of ourselves and others, and the relationships we have with them.

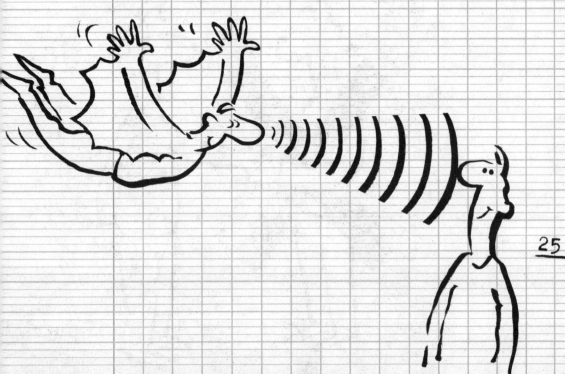

There are four positions of life: three show disruption to self-esteem:

1. I don't accept me but I accept others (- +)

This position is the result of difficulties in childhood a style of education and overprotection that is too permissive or too strict and demanding. Such a person or reaching adulthood won't have confidence in him or herself, nor in others. This person admires others but believes he/she is not able to do what they can do. This person is often anxious and sometimes depressive.

2. I accept myself but I don't accept others (+ -)

When a child hasn't had the security and care necessary for a harmonious upbringing, but had to 'fight to exist', on reaching adulthood this person becomes hard and distrustful of others. This can also happen when a child wasn't given kind and firm limits. The child then grows up to be godless and lawless and eventually treats others as if they were his or her slaves. This behaviour can appear at first to be 'high self-esteem', which is not really the case. It's about an attitude that shows a deep disturbance in self-esteem.

3. *I don't accept myself and I don't accept others (- -)*

This position reflects a serious lack of self-esteem. 'What's the good of this?' 'Anyway, we're going to be had.' 'It's not even worth trying!' 'All those idiots!'

People like this have a great deal of anger in them, against the world in general. They don't see any sense to their lives.

This behaviour can first appear as 'high self-esteem', which of course isn't really the case. It's about an attitude that shows a deep disturbance in self-esteem.

4. I accept myself, I recognise my value and I accept others and their values (+ +)

People like this have a good estimation of themselves. Their internal dialogue is positive. Faced with a new challenge their internal voice says: 'You're going to make it, you've got the skills, get on with it!'

For those who live in this position, it is possible for them to live fully, both accepting their lesser points and their good ones. They are capable of openness, of listening and of realism.

29

What are your positions in your chosen life?

Put a circle around your answers to the following eight questions:

Self-assessment of the positions of life[1]

On each of the eight themes in your public life below, rate yourself for each example on a scale from 0 to 10 according to the frequency with which you act like this.

1. Style of giving orders
  a. I justify myself, I defend myself, sometimes I criticise, somtimes I protect myself. **10**
  b. I use control and persuasion. I don't hesitate to use pressure. **0**
  c. I help people. My empathy helps me to be accepted. **9**
  d. I inform, I suggest opportunities for development, we analyse problems and opportunities together. **2**

2. Approach to problems
  a. I try to sidestep them, I organise myself. **8**
  b. I stick to the objectives and the quality of working life of each person. **4**
  c. Above all I'm careful to uphold the objectives. **4**
  d. I work so that everyone can feel satisfied. **4**

30

1 Test taken from *Transactional analysis and work relations,* Dominique Chalvin et al., 1979.

3. Attitude to rules
a. For me, rules are rules, that's all.   8
b. Rules are important. I make sure that they are followed.   8
c. There are rules of conduct. They're useful but we mustn't be their prisoners.   8
d. I think you have to force yourself to follow them.   4

4. View of conflicts
a. Conflicts can be useful. Sometimes we need them to make progress.   8
b. I don't really like conflicts, they're harmful to relationships.   8
c. I think you must first think of work and not reinvent the world.   2
d. It's not my business.   2

5. Reaction to anger
a. I don't like to face up to anger, it's painful for me.   2
b. It makes me very grumpy and distrustful.   10
c. When it comes to anger, I'm good at confrontation.   8
d. I wish it on those who take liberties, I brood on my resentment.   0

6. Attitude towards superiority
a. I see weak points easily, I criticise or I manipulate.   0
b. I do my best. I hope to be appreciated.   10
c. Each to his own work.   10
d. We discuss, we exchange, we negotiate.   10

7. Sense of humour
a. I laugh at my own expense.   10
b. I use irony to cover disappointment.   2
c. I know how to find the word that opens up and diffuses a situation.   4
d. My sense of humour is caustic and biting.   0

8. Basic attitude
a. I'll go along with you!   10
b. I'll get to the front with you!   6
c. I'll go because I have to.   8
d. Go there, go anywhere!   8

The results

	+ +	+ -	- +	- -
1. Style of giving orders	d 2	b 0	c 9	a 10
2. Approach to problems	b 4	c 4	d 4	a 8
3. Attitude to rules	c 8	b 8	d 4	a 8
4. View of conflicts	a 8	c 2	b 8	d 2
5. Reaction to anger	c 8	d 0	a 2	b 10
6. Attitude as a subordinate	d 6	a 10	b 2	c 4
7. Sense of humour	c 4	d 6	a 10	b 2
8. Basic attitude	b 6	a 10	c 8	d 8
Your total points	46	40	47	52

In general, we have a dominant position, and a secondary one that we use in situations of stress.

For a moment of relaxation, settle yourself comfortably
and let your eyes float to the centre of this endless
Tibetan knot.

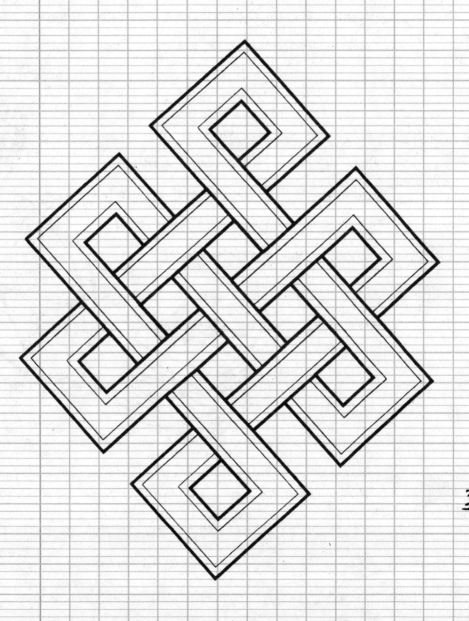

33

Self-esteem and procrastination

Another aspect of life that affects self-esteem is what we call **procrastination**, which means putting off until tomorrow what we could do today.

Current researchers in the field of self-esteem have shown that the ability to control and discipline yourself are the principal factors in having good self-esteem.

Procrastination comes from a lack of self-discipline. So do what has to be done immediately to increase your self-esteem.

Are you a 'procrastinator'? To find out, do the follow-
ing test:

	Not at all 0	Sometimes 1	Moderately 2	Frequently 3
I often say I'll do it when I want to do it.				✓
It annoys me when things are difficult.		✓		
I postpone deadlines when I don't feel like working.	✓			
I prefer to do nothing rather than do something and fail.			✓	
I'm very fussy about what I do.				✓
I'm never proud of my performances.		✓		
I dread not making it.				✓
I feel guilty when I think of everything I should be doing.				✓
I've never wanted to do what I have to do.	✓			
0. I hate people who try to control me and tell me what I should do.				✓ _35_

otal

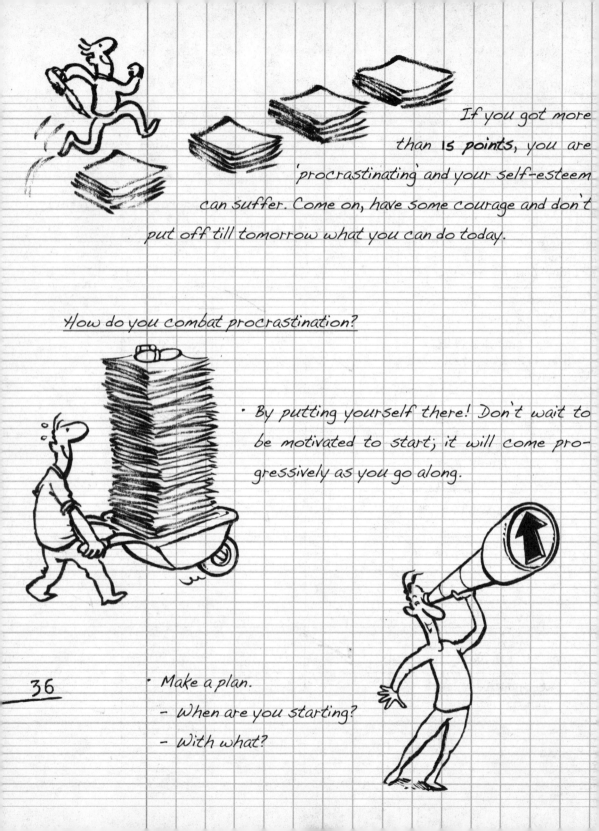

If you got more than **15 points**, you are 'procrastinating' and your self-esteem can suffer. Come on, have some courage and don't put off till tomorrow what you can do today.

How do you combat procrastination?

• By putting yourself there! Don't wait to be motivated to start; it will come progressively as you go along.

• Make a plan.
  - When are you starting?
  - With what?

· Break down the job into short stages of 15-20 minutes each, and off you go!

· Think positively. Identify negative sentences that you use and replace them with positive ones. For example, instead of

> 'Oh dear! I really don't want to do that!'

say instead:

> 'I'm going to do it for 20 minutes;
> today I feel full of energy!'

· Well done, give yourself a pat on the back.

Here's a little test

In the left-hand column write five things that you have the strongest desire to put off until tomorrow. Then, in the right-hand column write five excuses that you use to get out of doing them:

1.   1.

2.   2.

3.   3.

4.   4.

5.   5.

Don't wait any longer, give yourself the pleasure of colouring in this mandala.

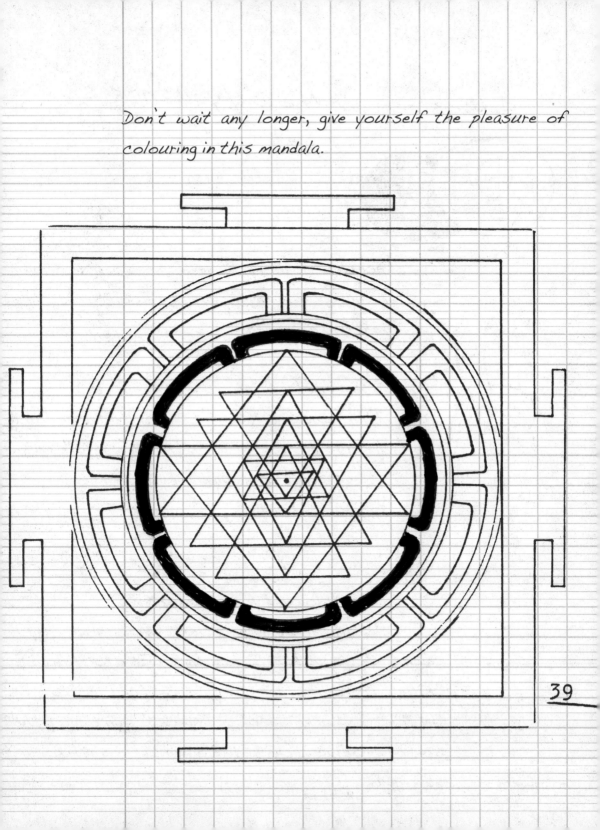

39

Self-esteem and the way you think

Recent psychological developments have shown the importance of the way a person thinks. Here are a few examples:

Use a mental filter

This concerns letting yourself be trapped in a negative point of view so that you ignore positive aspects. Consequently you devalue a positive point of view.

Example:

How did your Sunday go?

'Terrible! It rained, my roast was overcooked, they didn't like the pudding I'd made, it was a total flop!'

In fact there had been a shower, nobody had noticed the roast and only one of the guests hadn't eaten the pudding because he didn't like sugary things at the end of a meal.

- Using words such as 'should', 'shouldn't', 'have to' and 'must'

  These give you a feeling of being controlled from 'outside' yourself, whereas words like 'I decide' and 'I choose' would increase your self-esteem.

- Labelling yourself

  When you've made a mistake, you call yourself an 'idiot' or a 'fool' instead of simply accepting that you've made a mistake.

- Alocating blame

  'It's my fault, I should have known that it would rain! It's my fault, I bring bad luck wherever I go!'

  Or, blaming others without realising that you are also part of the problem. 'It's all the fault of my parents, they didn't give me the love that I should have had!'

- Becoming the victim

  'It isn't me, it's because of them, it's their fault, there was nothing else I could have done, it's normal to drink too much at a wedding ...', etc.

  Good self-esteem is incompatible with being a victim.

41

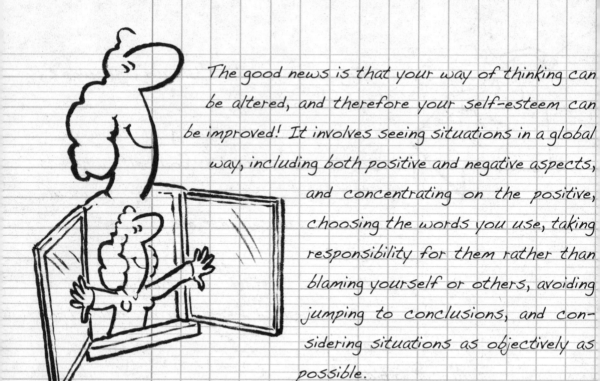

The good news is that your way of thinking can be altered, and therefore your self-esteem can be improved! It involves seeing situations in a global way, including both positive and negative aspects, and concentrating on the positive, choosing the words you use, taking responsibility for them rather than blaming yourself or others, avoiding jumping to conclusions, and considering situations as objectively as possible.

'It's all about learning your internal languages. An enormous part of your life takes place inside you and yourself. This has to be thoroughly explored so that you can choose the best bit!'

— Jean-Louis Servan-Schreiber

GOLD MINE

Self-esteem is above all a question of perception and interpretation of reality.

Event taking place

Perception and **interpretation**
of this event

Emotions that you feel
directly because of this event
(there can be many according to
how you interpret the event)

Behaviour, actions
(including actions in response to your emotions)

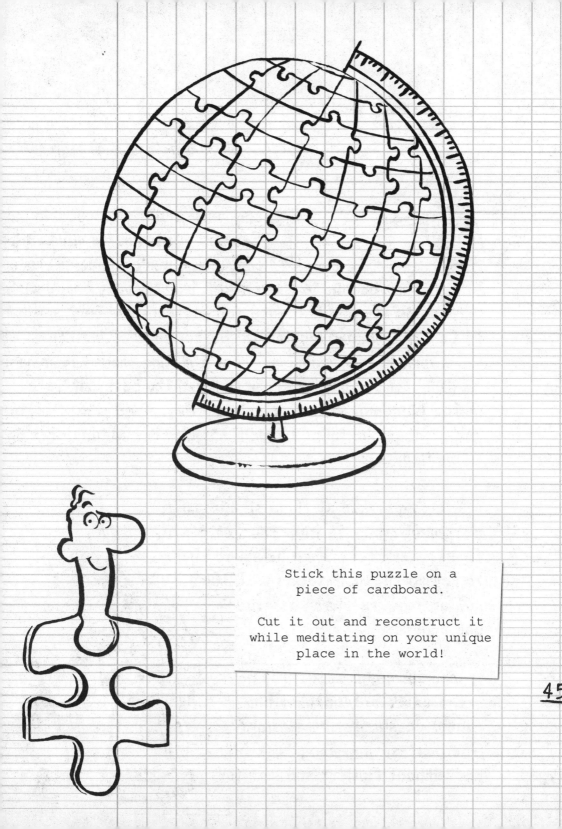

Stick this puzzle on a
piece of cardboard.

Cut it out and reconstruct it
while meditating on your unique
place in the world!

45

Dare to be yourself

Tang was a little worker in an Eastern kingdom. He worked in copper and made wonderful tools that he sold in the market. He was very happy with his life and had good self-esteem. He only wanted to find the woman who would be the love of his life.

One day, it was announced that the king wished to marry his daughter to the young man who had the best self-esteem in the kingdom. On the appointed day, Tang went to the palace where he found himself among several hundreds of young hopefuls.

The king looked at them all and asked his chamberlain to give each of them five flower seeds. Then he asked them to return the next spring with the pot of flowers that the seeds had produced.

Tang sowed his seeds, taking great care, but nothing happened, no shoots, no flowers. The next spring, Tang took his pot without flowers and left for

the palace. All the hundreds of young hopefuls carried pots full of fantastic flowers and they made fun of Tang, who had none.

Then the king asked each of them to come before him and present their pot. Tang came, a little nervous, before the king: 'Not a single seed germinated, your majesty', he said. The king replied, 'Tang, stay beside me'.

When all the young hopefuls had filed by, the king sent all of them away, except Tang. He announced to his kingdom that Tang and his daughter would be married the next summer. What an amazing party! Tang and the princess grew more and more in love with each other. They were extremely happy.

One day, Tang asked the king, his father-in-law: 'Majesty, how was it that you chose me for your son-in-law even though my seeds hadn't germinated?'

'Because they couldn't,' replied the king, 'I'd already boiled them for a whole night! However, you were the only one to have enough esteem of yourself to be honest! It was that sort of man I wanted for my son-in-law!'

Game of seven mistakes

Find the seven differences in the picture below.

Answers

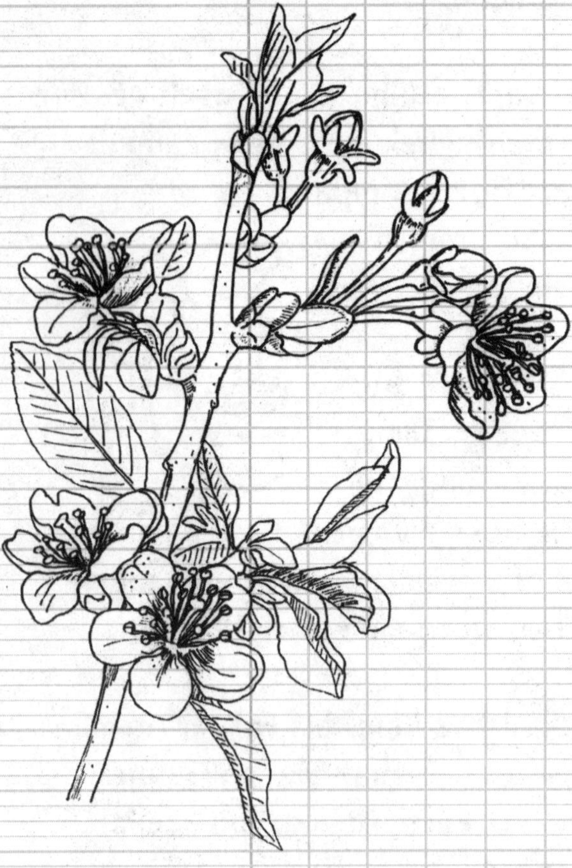

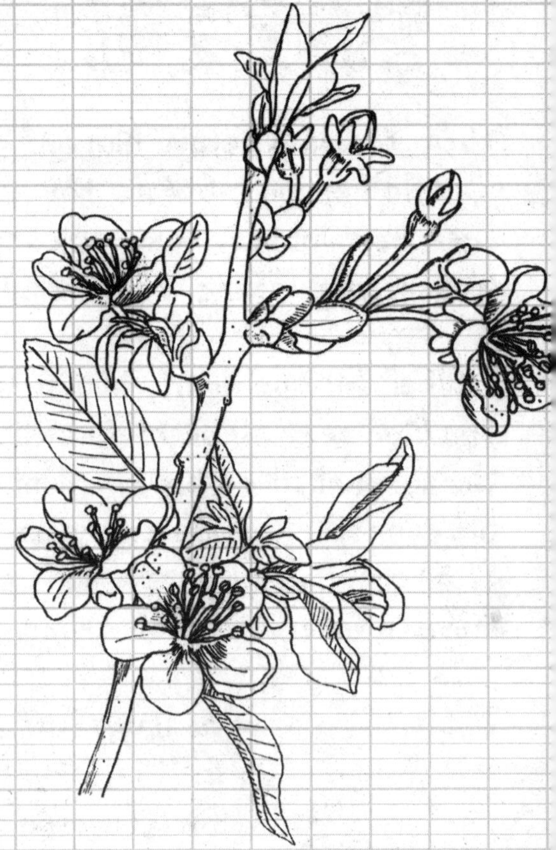

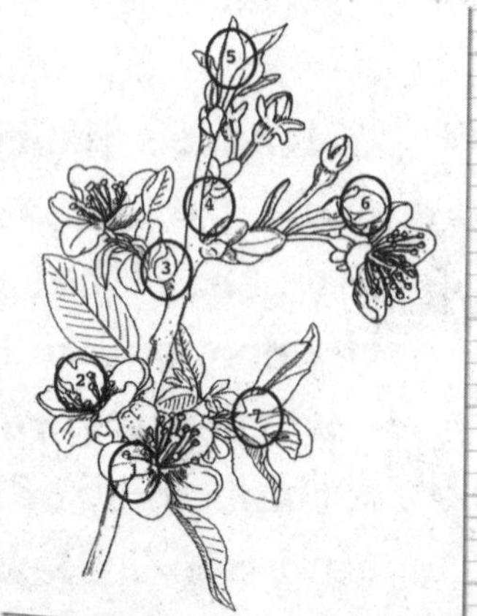

Increase your self-esteem

When you've understood what self-esteem is, as well as how it can be altered, it only remains for you to get on with it and take responsibility for the personal change that you want to effect.

Without doubt our parents and educators have given us important elements, both positive and negative. But having become adults, only we can make the decision to change and it's our responsibility to do so. This involves the following:

• To strengthen the belief in yourself that you have value as a person.

Have a positive view of yourself. Here's an exercise for this: below, write down five qualities that describe you:

1.

2.

3.

4.

5.

What qualities do your friends see in you?

1.

2.

3.

4.

5.

What quality, among those you've just specified, add most to your estimation of yourself?

...

Describe a situation or a moment in your life when you felt proud of yourself.

...

...

...

...

What is the most positive message that your parents, or anyone in that position, have given you?

...

...

...

What unique thing do you bring to humanity?

...

...

...

...

How would you want to be remembered after your death?

...

...

...

...

- Give up perfectionism in yourself and in others, meaning:

  'I have the right to do well but nobody
  has the right to ask me to be perfect'

- Take care with friend and family connections; develop your
  relationships with those who are emotionally strong.   51

- Learn to communicate in a clear and open way with others.

How many people do you have close to you, whom you understand and in whom you can confide without fear? Write their names at the end of the lines.

- Recognise the most important items in your interior dialogue.
  When you take the wrong road, what do you say to yourself?

  ...

  ...

  ...

  ...

  When you thank someone for having paid you a compliment, what do you say to yourself?

  ...

  ...

  ...

  ...

  Someone asks you to do something for them; you don't really want to say yes, but you do it all the same. What do you say to yourself about yourself?

  ...

  ...

  ...

  ...

53

You wake up late because your alarm clock didn't go off.
What do you say about yourself?

...

...

...

...

You have to have a medical examination and wait for the
results. What do you say to yourself?

...

...

...

...

...

You try on a new dress or jacket. What do you say to
yourself?

...

...

...

...

...

54

A close friend forgets your birthday. What do you say
to yourself?

...

...

...

...

...

Your child or teenager answers you back. What do you
say to yourself about yourself?

...

...

...

...

...

Is your interior dialogue more negative than positive?
How can you change it?

...

...

55

...

...

...

• Honour your own values

This assumes that you have identified them and affirmed them!

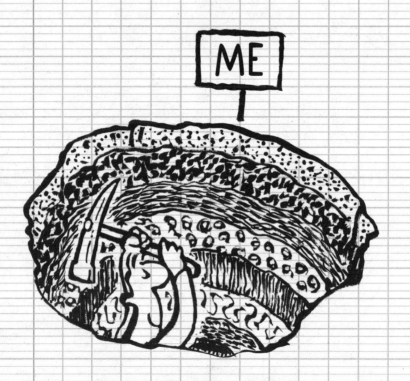

Settle yourself comfortably and concentrate on your breathing.

Repeat to yourself several times:

56

'I breathe in, I feel calm, I breathe out, I feel good ...'

When you're really relaxed, think of a very important value for you, one that you wish to embody in your personal life.

Visualise this value.

Now, visualise it inside you.

See how you put it into practice in your life.

Think of a situation in which you've experienced this value.

Feel the wellbeing that you felt on that occasion.

Recognise your ability to put this value in concrete form.

Congratulate yourself for having done that.

Then, return to your normal way of breathing.

And open your eyes.

You can do the same exercise with another value at any time.

Dare to be proud of yourself!

- It's also about strengthening the conviction that you do have the skills that enable you to face life.
  - to face changes rather than refuse them
  - to face up to conflicts rather than avoid them
  - to take calculated risks rather than always choosing security
  - to give up putting off doing things, instead doing today what can be done today
  - to know your personal strengths and resources.

Name 10 personal strengths that you recognise in yourself:

1.

2.

3.

4.

5.

6.

7.

8.

9.

10.

What positive statements can you write down that encourage you? Short positive statements starting with 'I ...'.

Example: 'I know that stress must be handled calmly.'

...

...

...

...

...

What are your main resources, internal or external?

...

...

...

...

...

What do you usually succeed in doing?

...

...

59

...

...

Name several successes in your life (of which you were the originator):

...

...

...

...

...

'One becomes what one thinks,
 one becomes what one sees,
 one becomes what one hears,
 one becomes what one loves.'

— Rosette Poletti

Cut out the following statements and choose one of them each day.

Today, I accept whatever happens	Today, I forgive	Today, I let go of my resistance
Today, I'm confident	Today, I thank someone	Today, I let go of my doubts
Today, I feel confident in myself	Today, I have a completely open mind	Today, I'm saying yes
Today, I blame nobody	Today, I'm throwing out my clutter	Today, I'm giving myself new freedom
Today, I'm letting go of an unnecessary rule	Today, I accept that I'm not perfect	Today, I give without expecting something in return
Today, I'm concentrating on love	**Today is a wonderful day to be alive**	Today is the only day that counts

In conclusion

Throughout the pages, excercises and reflections in this little book of exercises for self-esteem, we hope that you have advanced towards the objective of becoming fully what you can be, of offering to the human community this little bit of the essential puzzle that represents the destiny of men and women, that is yours.

To be all that you can be is to give yourself healthy self-esteem. It continues throughout your life, because each day brings its challenges to meet, difficulties to overcome and pleasures to be enjoyed!

We wish a safe journey to each of you who is concerned with the development of your self-esteem and that of those around you.

Good luck!

Rosette Poletti and Barbara Dobbs

63

Rosette Poletti and **Barbara Dobbs** are health professionals, nursing specialists and teachers of health and related issues.